I0933718

A LOVE DEVOUT
The True Untold Story of Mary Magdalene

Written by Paula Lawlor

MERCI
SAINTE MARIE-MADELEINE

PAUL VELLA HABER
MALTA
1995

A LOVE DEVOUT
The True Untold Story of Mary Magdalene

Written by Paula Lawlor

Magdalene Publishing

DEL MAR, CALIFORNIA
U.S.A.

ISBN 978-0-9830955-0-7

Printed in China

Book designed by Paula Lawlor

Visit www.MagdalenePublishing.org to purchase this book.

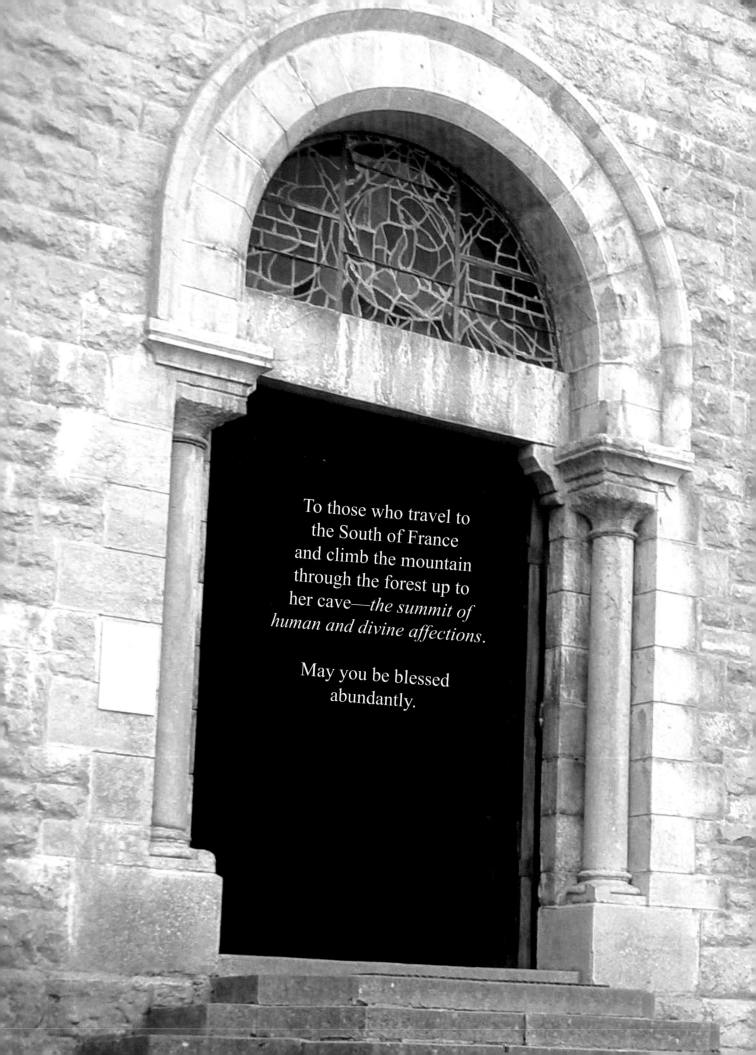

To those who travel to
the South of France
and climb the mountain
through the forest up to
her cave—*the summit of
human and divine affections.*

May you be blessed
abundantly.

Mary Magdalene
Apostle to the Apostles

Perhaps no figure in history is as controversial or mysterious as Mary Magdalene.

Mary Magdalene was a devout follower of Jesus. She accompanied Him during His travels and followed Him to the very end. She was present on Golgotha at the moment of Jesus' Crucifixion. While all the other disciples of Jesus ran away, she remained fearlessly at the cross together with other women, His Mother and the Apostle John.

She was faithful to Him not only in the days of His glory, but also at the moment of His extreme humiliation and agony. She was present at Jesus' burial. She watched as Joseph of Arimathea and Nikodemos went out to the tomb with His lifeless body; she watched as they covered over the entrance to the cave with a large stone, behind which went the Son of God.

While it was still dark Easter Sunday morning, Mary Magdalene went to the tomb to anoint His body. She found that the large stone was moved and the tomb was empty. According to all four gospels she was the first to witness the Resurrection

Door of the tabernacle on the main altar of *La Madeleine* in Paris, France depicts that first Easter morning when Mary Magdalene met Jesus in the garden, risen and alive outside the empty tomb.

of Jesus Christ and the first to announce His Resurrection to the apostles. Accordingly, she is referred to in early Christian writings as *"the apostle to the apostles."* She was a visionary and leader of the early movement who was so very dear to the Heart of Jesus.

Mary Magdalene is a saint in the Catholic Church, and is a saint as well in the Eastern Orthodox, Gregorian and Anglican churches. Her feast day is July 22nd.

Pope Gregory's Homily of Mary Magdalene

Since the late 6th century, Mary Magdalene has been identified in Western Christian Tradition as an adulteress and repentant prostitute.

On September 14, 591, Pope Gregory I (Gregory the Great) gave a powerful homily at Saint Clements Basilica in Rome in which he stated that he believed: "that the woman Luke called a sinner (Luke 7:37) and John called Mary (John 11:2 and 12:3) was the Mary out of whom Mark declared that seven demons were cast (Mark 16:9)" *(Hanc vero quam Lucas peccatricem mulierem, Joannes Mariam nominat, illam esse Mariam credimus de qua Marcus septem damonia ejecta fuisse testatur).*[1]

Pope Gregory's 33rd homily in 591 is actually responsible for Mary Magdalene's shameful reputation:

Luke 7:37-38 - "And behold, a woman in the city who was a sinner, when she knew that Jesus sat at the table in the Pharisee's house, brought an alabaster flask of fragrant oil, and stood at His feet behind Him weeping; and she began to wash His feet with her tears, and wiped them with the hair of her head; and she kissed His feet and anointed them with the fragrant oil."

Feast in the House of Simon by Sandro Botticelli (c.1484-9), Philadelphia Museum of Art.

John 11:2 - "It was that Mary who anointed the Lord with fragrant oil and wiped His feet with her hair, whose brother Lazarus was sick."

John 12:1-3 - "Then six days before the Passover, Jesus came to Bethany, where Lazarus was who had been dead, whom He had raised from the dead. There they made Him a supper; and Martha served, but Lazarus was one of those who sat at the table with Him. Then Mary took a pound of very costly oil of spikenard, anointed the feet of Jesus, and wiped His feet with her hair. And the house was filled with the fragrance of the oil."

Mark 16:9 - "Now when He rose

early on the first day of the week, He appeared first to Mary Magdalene, out of whom He had cast seven demons."

Mary Magdalene is mentioned in all four gospels, but nowhere is she described as a prostitute. This image of Mary comes from confusion between Mary Magdalene in Mark's gospel (Mark 16:9), Mary, Martha's sister and an unnamed sinner in Luke's gospel (Luke 7:36-50). Pope Gregory the Great declared that all three women were the same person and his focus was on *Mary the sinner*.

In John's gospel (John 8:3-11), Jesus stops a crowd from stoning a woman for prostitution. There is no indication in the text that either unnamed woman is Mary Magdalene, but tradition has linked the prostitute with Mary Magdalene:

John 8:3-11 - "Then the scribes and Pharisees brought to Him a woman caught in adultery. And when they had set her in the midst, they said to Him, 'Teacher, this woman was caught in adultery, in the very act. Now Moses, in the law, commanded us that such should be stoned. But what do You say?' This they said, testing Him, that they might have something of which to accuse Him. But Jesus stooped down and wrote on the ground with His finger, as though He did not hear. So when they continued asking Him, He raised Himself up and said to them, 'He who is without sin among you, let him throw a stone at her first.' And again He stooped down and wrote on the ground. Then those who heard it, being convicted by their conscience, went out one by one, beginning with the oldest even to the last. And Jesus was left alone, and the woman standing in the midst. When Jesus had raised himself up and saw no one but the woman, He said to her, 'Woman, where are those accusers of yours? Has no one condemned you?' She said, 'No one, Lord.' And Jesus said to her, 'Neither do I condemn you; go and sin no more.'"

The traditional Roman Catholic feast day (July 22nd) dedicated to St. Mary Magdalene celebrated her position as a penitent. In 1969, the Catholic Church clarified that Mary Magdalene's image as a reformed prostitute is not supported by the text of the Bible and it revised the Roman Missal and the Roman Calendar, and now her feast day is celebrated with the gospel of the Resurrection where Mary Magdalene was the first to see the Risen Lord and was told by Him to go and tell the apostles.

The Provençal Tradition

There is a widely recognized, time-honored alliance between Mary Magdalene and Provence. Two significant sites of pilgrimage bear witness to this claim: the Basilica of Saint Mary Magdalene in *St. Maximin-la-Sainte-Baume* and the Sainte Baume, a mountain cave on the plain of the *Plan d'Aups*, overlooking the *Massif de la Sainte-Baume*.

Tradition has it that, after the execution of St. James in Jerusalem (son of Zebedee and Mary Salome), Mary Magdalene, her sister Martha and brother Lazarus were persecuted by the Jews of Jerusalem and imprisoned. The Jews were afraid of the crowd if they were to execute the prisoners so they towed them off the shores of Palestine in a boat without sails or oars or supplies and abandoned them to the open sea. Others in the boat included Mary Jacobe, mother of James and the sister of the Virgin Mary, Mary Salome, mother of the apostles James and John, Maximin, one of the seventy two disciples of Christ, Cedonius, the blind man who was miraculously healed by Jesus, Marcelle, Martha's servant,

Low relief, in gold-leafed wood, from the altar of the Rosary in the Basilica of Saint Mary Magdalene, depicts Mary Magdalene and her companions being sent off to sea.

and Sara, maid of the two Marys.

After narrowly escaping death during a storm at sea the boat finally came to shore on the coast of Gaul in a town now called *Saintes-Maries-de-la-Mer* in Camargue.

Mary Jacobe, Mary Salome and Sara remained in Camargue. Martha traveled towards Avignon and ended up in Tarascon. Mary Magdalene, Lazarus, Maximin and Cedonius traveled on to Marseille where Mary Magdalene began to preach. They ended up converting the whole of Provence. Lazarus became the first bishop of Marseille. Mary Magdalene then went on to Aix where Maximin had already gone, some twenty miles north of Marseille.

Baume was built in memory of Mary Magdalene being raised by angels.

When the time of Mary Magdalene's death arrived she was carried by angels to the oratory of Maximin, where she received viaticum. She died in Maximin's arms and her body was laid in an alabaster sarcophagus in an oratory he constructed in the Gallo Roman town of Villa Latta or Tégulata, which after Maximin's death became St. Maximin.

Mary Magdalene Preaching in Marseille (c. 1518), Philadelphia Museum of Art.

Maximin became the first bishop of Aix and Mary Magdalene retreated to a mountain cave on the plain of the *Plan d'Aups* known as Sainte Baume (47 AD) where she remained alone for the last thirty years of her life in contemplation, prayer and penance. She is said to have been lifted up by the angels seven times each day at the canonical hours and fed heavenly nourishment. The tiny chapel of Saint Pilon on the crest above Sainte

Mary Magdalene's Last Communion by Sandro Botticelli (c. 1484-9), Philadelphia Museum of Art.

Maximin, Cedonius and Marcelle are buried at St. Maximin. Mary Jacobe, Mary Salome and Sara are buried in Notre Dame de la Mer in Saintes-Maries-de-la-Mer. Martha is buried in St. Martha's Church in Tarascon and Lazarus is buried in the Abbey of St. Victor in Marseille.

History of Sainte Baume & Saint Maximin

Since prehistoric times the Sainte Baume was known as the Sacred Mountain of Marseille. It was a place of worship of fertility which included the Artemis of Ephesus. Around 60 AD the Roman poet Lucan, nephew of Seneca, mentions a "sacred grove" near Marseille...

In 414 John Cassian, a native of Marseille who had just spent time in Egypt, returned to "Provincia Romana" (Provence) and founded the Abbey of St. Victor over the grave of Saint Lazarus in Marseille. This complex of monasteries for both men and women was one of the first such institutes in the west, and served as a model for later monastic development. In 415 Cassian founded a monastery in St. Maximin and chose Saint Mary Magdalene as a patron and model for his monks and nuns. The cave of Sainte Baume was inaccessible at that time so the Cassianites built a path and stairs so that pilgrims could go up. The Cassian monks were the guards of Mary Magdalene's relics and remained so until 1079.

A *Life of Mary Magdalene* was known in the early seventh century because Saint Didier (590-655), bishop of Cahors, wrote of it in a letter to Abbess Aspasia to encourage her to stay constant in her conversion.

In 710 with the arrival of the Saracens, interspersed with incursions by Charles Martel's band, atrocities were committed that, according to the Tradition, drove the guardians of Mary Magdalene's relics to transfer her remains to another crypt and con-

It was the Cassianites who originally built a path and stairs so that pilgrims could go up to the Sainte Baume to see the cave where Mary Magdalene spent the last thirty years of her life.

ceal it, burying memory still deeper.

Raban Maur (780-856), Abbot of the Benedictine Abbey at Fuld for twenty years and then archbishop of Mainz, wrote *The Life of St. Martha and St. Mary Magdalen*. Raban Maur was a man of great knowledge and was extremely pious. With his influence and dignity he was one of the most considerable men of his time. Raban Maur followed the gospels step by step, and when the gospel ended with the Ascension of Jesus Christ, he used ancient writings as the foundation for his manuscript. The following few paragraphs are a brief portion of an account of this ancient tale as given by Rabanus Maurus (*Dublin Review*, July 1878):

"Now, in the fourteenth year after the Ascension the Apostles separated; and when St. Peter was about to leave the East to go to Rome, he chose from among the older and more faithful companions of the Savior, those who were to carry the Gospel to the West, whither he could not go himself; and first of these was the learned Maximin, one of the seventy-two disciples and illustrious for the gift of working miracles. St. Mary Magdalen, who was bound by ties of charity to this disciple, determined never to leave him wherever he might be called to go: and there were other illustrious women and widows, who had ministered to the disciples at Jerusalem, and who would follow St. Magdalen out of love for her wherever she went. Therefore, in the company of Magdalen, the glorious friend of God, and of St. Martha, her sister, the holy Bishop Maximin took ship and abandoned himself to the mercy of the waves. And so, driven by the winds, they left the coast of Asia, going down by the Tyrrhenian Sea; and leaving Italy on their right hand, they were happily driven ashore on the coast of Viennese Gaul, nigh to the city, Marseilles, where the Rhône casts itself into the sea."

The wide, uninterrupted plain stretching from Arles to the sea, including the delta of the Rhône, or the triangular space between its two branches is the island of Camargue. There is only one village in Camargue, Saintes Maries. Its name comes from Saint Mary Salome, Saint Mary Jacobe and Saint Mary Magdalene landing on the adjoining coast.[2] There is an annual gathering in the town of *Saintes-Maries-de-la-Mer*. May 24th is Sara's Procession (the patron saint of the Gypsies) and May 25th is a procession to venerate the memories of the three saints.

Among the writings which Raban Maur referenced is *Apostolic Life* which dates back to the 5th or 6th century. The fact that his manuscript is authentic has been confirmed by a collection of letters that in the archaeological world inspire confidence.

The 9th century manuscript bearing the name Raban Maur, *The Life of St. Martha and of St. Mary Magdalen,* can be found at Magdalen College, at Oxford University, England - a college dedicated to Saint Mary Magdalene.

Half a century had gone by since the hiding of the relics. The Saracens were defeated and those who knew the place of hiding had passed away. Devotion to the great penitent burst forth. Pope Stephen II in 816 and Pope John VIII in 878 paid visits to St. Maximin and Sainte Baume.

In 1030 the Benedictine monastery at Vézelay, in Burgundy, announced the news that the relics of Saint Mary Magdalene had been discovered and that they were with them. A rivalry began between St. Maximin and Vézelay.

In 1254, returning from the seventh Crusade, Saint Louis, king of France, on hearing of La Sainte Baume, greatly desired to visit it with his knights; this royal pilgrimage ended up having great repercussions.

In 1279, St. Louis' nephew, Charles II (Prince of Salerno and Count of Provence) acquired knowledge that the relics were buried in the town of St. Maximin at the church with the same name, so he ordered excavations in Saint Maximin to search for them. On December 10, 1279, deep in the earth, he found the marble tomb. When he tried to open it a wonderful smell of perfume filled the air. Inside lay her entire body except her jaw bone. In the dust inside the tomb was a wooden tablet wrapped in wax:

Hic requiescit magdalenae corpus Mariae.

Translation of the inscription on the wooden tablet: "Here lies the body of Mary Magdalene."

"Here lies the body of Mary Magdalene" and a parchment which explained that in 710 her remains had been secretly transferred during the night into the marble tomb of Cedonius and hidden so that the Saracens wouldn't find them.

In the year of the Birth of our Lord, 710, the sixth day of December, the reign of Eudes, the very good King of the French, at the time of the ravages of the treacherous people, the Saracens, this body of the very dear and holy St. Mary Magdalen, out of fear of the said treacherous people, has been secretly translated during the night from the alabaster tomb to this one, which is marble, since here it is more hidden and from which the body of St. Sidonius has been withdrawn.[3]

English translation of the Latin inscription on the parchment "about the size of a man's palm," wrapped in bark that was found in the tomb next to the human remains of Saint Mary Magdalene.

On April 6, 1295 the skull was reunited with its jaw bone at St. John Lateran in Rome where it had been venerated for centuries, thanks to Pope Boniface VIII, who then published the pontifical bull for the establishment of the Dominicans at Sainte Baume and St. Maximin.

Some years later the *Basilica of Saint Mary Magdalene* was built over the spot where Charles II found her remains. A Dominican priory was built in St. Maximin as well as a little priory at Sainte Baume. Vézelay's claim of possessing the holy relics faded away.

Since then hundreds of thousands of pilgrims, including many kings and popes and saints, have continued to journey to Sainte Baume and St. Maximin to pray and to give thanks for the intercession of Saint Mary Magdalene.

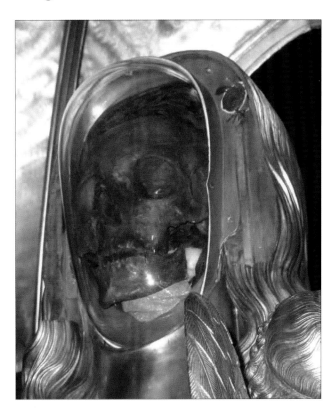

Today the skull of Saint Mary Magdalene along with her jaw bone are in a gold reliquary in the *Basilica of Saint Mary Magdalene* in St. Maximin.

ALPES-DE-
HAUTE-
PROVENCE

Italie

Digne

ALPES-
MARITIMES

Castellane

Nice

Monaco

Grasse

Notre-Dame de Valcluse

Cap d'Antibes

VAR

Draguignan

Cannes

Côte d'Azur

Fréjus

Brignoles

Saint-Tropez

Mer Méditerranée

In 1781 Louis XVI had a piece of the bone extracted from the shrine in order to offer it to the Duke of Parma. Several decades later the Italians offered Louis XVIII parts of the relics, and in 1824 he gave them to the parish of *La Madeleine* in Paris.[4]

In 1793 during the French Revolution the shrine was broken into and the relics thrown about. The Basilica at St. Maximin was saved from utter destruction by transforming it into a government store placing over the great door the words - *Fournitures Militaires*.

Joseph Bastide, sacristan of St. Maximin, removed the skull along with the *Sainte Ampoule* (the glass sphere containing earth soaked with blood of Jesus Christ collected by Mary Magdalene at the foot of the cross) and the vase holding the *noli me tangere* - the small piece of skin that was attached to the skull where Jesus touched her after His Resurrection. After the Revolution, Bastide brought his treasure to the archbishop. Lucien Bonaparte helped save the forest of Sainte Baume but the revolutionaries deliberately started a fire in the cave and destroyed what had been rebuilt after the fire of the fifteenth century.[5]

A portion of the tibia of the right leg and a lock of hair of Saint Mary Magdalene were rescued by Madame Ricard who fled to Bonnieux in fear and stayed with the Anselme family. These relics remained in the hands of the head of the household, Joseph Hyacinthe-Philippe d'Anselme and father of Louis-Victor d'Anselme and Marie-Marguerite-Félicité d'Anselme who married Jean-Baptiste Terris. From this marriage was born the last of eleven children, Joseph Sébastien Ferdinand Terris, on January 20, 1824. He was ordained a priest in 1847 and ordained bishop of Fréjus in 1876. He was given the relics of Saint Mary Magdalene which had been rescued during the French Revolution by Madame Ricard.

In 1878 Bishop Joseph Sébastien Ferdinand Terris of Fréjus offered the new Pope Leo XIII a fragment of these relics along with some of Saint Mary Magdalene's hair.

In 1884 Bishop Terris gave some of the relics belonging to Saint Mary Magdalene to the diocese of Fréjus. A reliquary was built by goldsmith Lyon Armand Caillat to contain a fragment of her right tibia and a lock of her hair which was to be kept as much as possible in the cave of Mary Magdalene - Sainte Baume, and was installed there in 1889.[6]

In 1889, this reliquary of Saint Mary Magdalene made by goldsmith Lyon Armand Caillat was installed in Sainte Baume. It contains a fragment of her right tibia and a lock of her hair.

From 1814 onwards, Sainte Baume was little by little rebuilt from its ashes until, in 1859, Father Henri Dominique Lacordaire, a Dominican monk, reinstalled the Dominican Order which had been faithful keepers and guides to pilgrims. Father Lacordaire wanted to give witness to the Gospel. He wrote in his study on Saint Mary Magdalene: "When the Son of God came to save men, nobody was astonished that the Gospel might be a book of love and Love the book of Salvation."

The Hôtellerie de la Sainte Baume on the plain below Sainte Baume at the edge of the forest was rebuilt in 1859 by Father Lacordaire. The Dominicans are installed there and continue to receive pilgrims throughout the year: www.hotellerie.sainte-baume.org

Father Lacordaire wanted Sainte Baume to speak the most of beautiful friendships: "This should be the summit of human and divine affections; Jesus Christ loved souls, and He passes on to us this love which was the basis of Christianity... It is friendship, love, that by which God became man and died for men, which could conceive of this."

Many people of this world have come on pilgrimage to Saint Baume; but the most memorable pilgrimages are those of the saints who have come to pray; 14 pilgrims are now canonized. Some of them include Saint Louis of France, Saint Bridgit of Sweden, Saint Catherine of Siena, and the beggar, Saint Benoît-Joseph Labre. An Algerian priest, Charles de Foucauld, spent long hours praying in Sainte Baume.[7] He was beatified by Pope Benedict XVI in November of 2005.

Father Marie-Etienne Vayssière was keeper of the cave from 1900 to 1932. He was responsible for rebuilding the staircase leading to the cave and lining it with a *Way of the Cross* and *Calvary*.

In July and August of 2004 Bishop Dominique Marie Jean Rey, from the diocese of Fréjus-Toulon, accompanied the relics of Saint Mary Magdalene that came from Sainte Baume to the cities of Sao Paulo and Fortaleza in Brazil where they were venerated by thousands of the faithful.

In August 2009 these same relics went on a pilgrimage for the purpose of evangelization to various cities in the diocese of Fréjus-Toulon as well as Toulouse, Lyon and Paris.

Bishop Dominique Rey gave his permission and the Sainte Baume relic of Saint Mary Magdalene went on its first tour of North America in October and November of 2009 ac-

companied by several French Dominicans from Sainte Baume.

The Sainte Baume relic of Saint Mary Magdalene was venerated from October 21st to November 30th in many different cities in the States of Georgia, Alabama, Mississippi, Louisiana, New York, Pennsylvania and Florida, and also in the nation's capitol, Washington, DC at *The Dominican House of Studies*. How fortunate were those who were able to take part in the blessed event.

In 2010 eight California bishops extended letters of invitation to the bishop of Fréjus-Toulon and the Sainte Baume Dominicans to carry Saint Mary Magdalene's relic to California for veneration in their respective diocese. A second United States tour of the relic, from mid-February to mid-March 2011, will enable Saint Mary Magdalene to continue to touch and convert the hearts of many.

For the purpose of the U.S. tour a new reliquary was built which contained the right tibia of Saint Mary Magdalene.

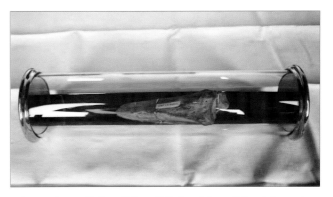

A portion of the tibia of Saint Mary Magdalene is enclosed in a glass tube and then placed in the reliquary.

Chapel
Saint Pilon

Cave of Saint Mary Magdalene
and the Dominican Abbey chiseled
into the rock-face

Calvary built by Father Vayssière is on the left, the Dominican Monastery is on the edge of the cliff on the right and the entrance to the cave of Saint Mary Magdalene, Sainte Baume, is in the middle.

The steep climb up to the cave of Saint Mary Magdalene from the Hôtellerie de la Sainte Baume on the plain below takes a good forty-five minutes to an hour. After leaving the plain, one makes their way up through the dense, mysterious and sacred forest which is unpenetrated by sunshine. In spite of the very old age of the trees, the Sainte Baume forest is well and living. The sounds of many different birds and other living creatures fill the air and accompany the pilgrims on their journey to the top.

Chapel Saint Pilon was built on the crest of the mountain in memory of Saint Mary Magdalene being raised up by angels seven times daily.

View is from the entrance of the cave. In front of the Rock of Penitence is the high altar, which is the work of Bossan (c. 1868). Mass is held daily in the cave at eleven o'clock in the morning. To the right of the altar and set back a distance it a statue of Saint Mary Magdalene being raised up by angels.

After a long steep climb traversing back and forth through the forest the pilgrim finally sees a glimpse of the Monastery at the top of the cliff. One then must climb many stairs to reach the entrance to the Monastery which displays an imitation of *Calvary* upon entering. A few more flights of stone stairs and one finally reaches the entrance to the cave. It is cold and moist inside. The cave is surprisingly large and remains quite natural as it was two thousand years ago. A stone wall with a large door and three stained glass windows on either side covers what must have

This beautiful statue of *Mary Magdalene raised up by angels* is the work of L. J. Alexandre (c. 1878). Pilgrims come from all over the world to her cave to pray: *"Marie Madeleine prier pour nous."*

light into the cave. A floor and stairs leading to the lower level have been added. Natural springs fill crevices in the cave with water.

The experience of being inside the cave is truly incredible. One can only imagine how it must have been for Mary Magdalene to have spent the last thirty years of her life there, alone.

been a huge opening. Seven beautiful stained glass windows and the opening of the entrance door allow some

Dominicans celebrating the feast day Mass at the Basilica of Saint Mary Magdalene in St. Maximin-la-Sainte-Baume (Sunday, July 26, 2009). After the feast day Mass there is a procession carrying the skull of Mary Magdalene in the gold reliquary through the streets of St. Maximin-la-Sainte-Baume. To the left is the monumental pulpit, in sculptured walnut, carved by the Dominican brother Louis Gudet (c. 1756).

The Basilica of Saint Mary Magdalene is located about twenty miles from Sainte Baume in the town of St. Maximin-la-Sainte-Baume. It is here on this ground that Saint Maximin buried her in an alabaster tomb. It is here where the Cassian monks hid her remains in the year 710. It is here where Charles II discovered her in the marble tomb and then built the magnificent monument over it for all the world to come and see.

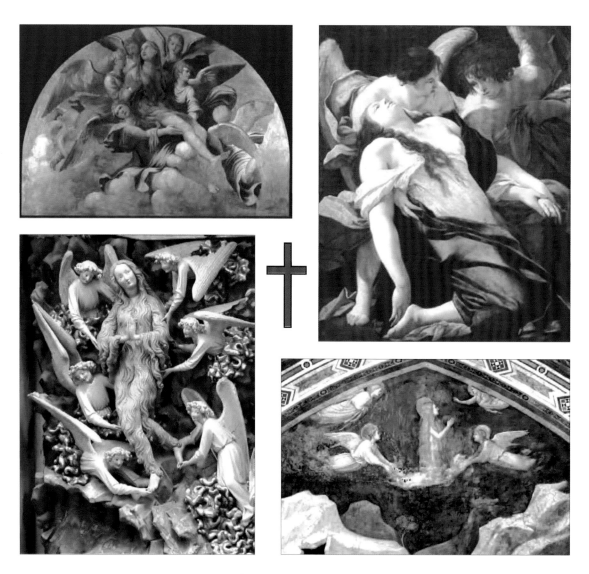

Mary Magdalene Carried by Angels

Tradition of Mary Magdalene being raised up by angels began with a monk who was living in a cave close to Sainte Baume who saw a woman being carried with regularity by angels. He also heard their beautiful singing. He prayed to God to understand what he had witnessed and one day the woman spoke to him. She asked him if he knew of the Mary Magdalene who accompanied Jesus during his travels. When he replied "yes," she explained that she was that Mary Magdalene and that she had been living in that cave for the last thirty years, and each day had been carried up by angels to receive nourishment and then carried back. Mary Magdalene then asked the monk to go down the mountain to the church in Tégulata where Maximin was and tell him that soon she would be coming to him because she was at the end of her life. The monk did as requested and the news of her coming to see Maximin pleased the bishop very much. Mary Magdalene later appeared with angels in Bishop Maximin's oratory where he gave her viaticum (food for the journey), and then she died in his arms.[8]

Paula Lawlor says an unexpected spiritual journey while visiting a dear friend in Cannes, France, led her to the cave of Mary Magdalene (*Sainte Baume*), a place she never knew existed. After praying to the Saint in the cave, and the very next day having her prayer answered, Paula made a second climb up the mountain through the forest to the cave to light another candle and give thanks for the miracle. Later in research she discovered the error made by Pope Gregory I in a powerful homily he delivered in Rome in the year 591, testifying: *"that the woman Luke called a sinner and John called Mary was the Mary out of whom Mark declared that seven demons were cast."* Pope Gregory's focus on *Mary the sinner* created confusion and a tradition that linked the prostitute with Mary Magdalene—despite the fact that there is no indication in the text of the gospel that the unnamed woman is Mary Magdalene.

Paula was inspired to write the book *A LOVE DEVOUT—The True Untold Story of Mary Magdalene* because of the miracle she received. "It is an expression of gratitude," she says and adds, "I also want to correct the misconception many have of this holy woman who was so very dear to the Heart of Jesus, and to make her accessible to all by laying a clear path to the cave in the South of France where she lived the last thirty years of her life—*Sainte Baume*."

Paula Lawlor, a researcher and writer, is a mother of seven and lives in Del Mar, California.

References

[1] Patrologia Latina, vol. 76 (Paris: J.-P. Migne, 1844-1864), *SANCTI GREGORII MAGNI, XL HOMILIARUM IN EVANGELIA LIB. II - HOMIL. XXXIII,* column 1239 (1592-1593) http://documentacatholicaomnia.eu/01p/0590-0604,_SS_Gregorius_I_Magnus,_Homiliarum_In_Evangelia_Libri_Duo,_MLT.pdf

[2] *A FORGOTTEN SHRINE,* Canon F. M. Ryan, The Irish Monthly, Seventh Yearly Volume, 1879, Dublin, Ireland http://books.google.com/books?id=6isEAAAAQAAJ&pg=PA369&dq=The+Irish+Monthly,+a+forgotten+shrine&cd=3 #v=onepage&q&f=false

[3] Ibid

[4] *the Church of la Madeleine—History of a parish*, François Pupil, imprimerie modern (Pont-à-Mousson 54), 2000

[5] *A FORGOTTEN SHRINE,* Canon F. M. Ryan, The Irish Monthly, Seventh Yearly Volume, 1879, Dublin, Ireland http://books.google.com/books?id=6isEAAAAQAAJ&pg=PA369&dq=The+Irish+Monthly,+a+forgotten+shrine&cd=3 #v=onepage&q&f=false

[6] *The Relics of Saint Marie-Magdalene at "La Sainte Baume,"* MARY MAGDALENE HISTORY (Diocese of Fréjus-Toulon, Southern France), by François Brenneur, October 2009   http://www.jp2trainingcenter.com/marymagdalenehistory

[7] *Since prehistoric times... Until 2002*, A quick overview of the prehistory and history of Sainte Baume, Sainte Baume Dominicain http://translate.googleusercontent.com/translate_c?hl=en&sl=fr&u=http://saintebaume.dominicains.com/spip.php%3Fart icle1&rurl=translate.google.com&usg=ALkJrhiPEApCpLn0lw1bIfBuA4Jo_Y6T9g

[8] *The GOLDEN LEGEND or LIVES of the SAINTS,* Compiled by Jacobus de Voragine, Archbishop of Genoa, 1275 First Edition Published 1470, Englished by William Caxton, First Edition 1483, Volume IV, *Life of S. Mary Magdalene* http://www.fordham.edu/halsall/basis/goldenlegend/GoldenLegend-Volume4.htm#Mary Magdalene

Photographs by Paula Lawlor—FRONT TO BACK

COVER—*Marie Madeleine* by R. Eischmaninoff (c. 1858), original painting Paula found at the Marché Forville, the outdoor antique market in Cannes, France

Statue of Saint Mary Magdalene on the altar inside Chapel Saint Pilon, on the crest of the Sainte Baume range

Sarcophagus of Saint Mary Magdalene in the crypt of the *Basilica of Saint Mary Magdalene*

Oratory of The Crucifixion—In 1516, Monseigneur Jean Ferrier II, Archbishop of Arles, had seven oratories erected along the "Chemin des Rois" (King's Way) from Nans les Pins to the summit of Saint Pilon evoking main events in the life of Saint Mary Magdalene. Today only four oratories remain.

DEDICATION—Entrance to *Sainte Baume*, the cave of Saint Mary Magdalene

Page 1—Tabernacle door on the high altar of *La Madeleine,* church dedicated to Saint Mary Magdalene in Paris, France

Page 2—Statue of Mary Magdalene lamenting over Jesus' death just across from the entrance to *Sainte Baume*

Page 3—Mary Magdalene washes Jesus' feet with her hair—*Feast in the House of Simon* by Sandro Botticelli (c. 1484-9), Philadelphia Museum of Art, John G. Johnson Collection

Page 5—Gold-leafed wood relief from the altar of the Rosary in the *Basilica of Saint Mary Magdalene* depicting Mary Magdalene and her companions being sent off to sea

Page 6—*Mary Magdalene Preaching in Marseille,* panel from an altarpiece (c. 1518), Philadelphia Museum of Art, John G. Johnson Collection

Page 6—Scene from the Legend of Mary Magdalene, *Mary Magdalene's Last Communion* by Sandro Botticelli (c. 1484-9), Philadelphia Museum of Art, John G. Johnson Collection

Photographs—CONTINUED

Page 7—Stairs originally built by the Cassianites leading to the cave of Saint Mary Magdalene

Page 10—Skull of Saint Mary Magdalene in the gold reliquary in the *Basilica of Saint Mary Magdalene*

Page 14—Reliquary containing a fragment of Mary Magdalene's right tibia and a lock of her hair in *Sainte Baume*

Page 14—Hôtellerie de la Sainte Baume

Page 15—*Jesus dies on the cross* - this twelveth station of the cross built by Father Marie-Etienne Vayssière was inaugurated in 1914, just a few days before the outbreak of the First World War.

Page 17—View from the plain below of the mysterious and sacred forest, the cave of Saint Mary Magdalene and the Dominican Abbey chiseled into the rock-face, and Chapel Saint Pilon

Page 18—Photo taken from the Hôtellerie de la Sainte Baume on the plain below - Calvary built by Father Vayssière on the left, the Dominican Monastery on the edge of the cliff on the right and the entrance to Sainte Baume, the cave of Mary Magdalene, in the middle

Page 18—Chapel Saint Pilon

Page 19—View of the inside of the cave of Saint Mary Magdalene (Sainte Baume) from the entrance door

Page 20—Statue of Mary Magdalene raised up by angels with seven candles below that Paula lit for each of her children when she prayed to the Saint the first time she visited *Sainte Baume*

Page 20—The stone staircase leading to the lower level of the cave with the statue of Mary Magdalene raised up by angels in the background on the first level

Page 21—Statue of Mary Magdalene holding the crucifix in the lower level of *Sainte Baume*

Page 22—Dominicans celebrating the 2009 feast day Mass at the *Basilica of Saint Mary Magdalene*

Page 24—*Ecstasy of Saint Mary Magdalene* by Charles Marochetti (1806-1868) took twelve years to complete, above the high altar in *La Madeleine*, a church dedicated to St. Mary Magdalene in Paris, France (marble height 449 cm)

LAST TWO PAGES—Inside the cave near the statue of *Mary Magdalene raised up by angels* and a close up of the far left candle Paula lit on her return to the cave to give thanks for the miracle. The miracle was for her son Francis, *"MERCI Marie Madeleine pour tous."* Note the feet of the angels lifting Mary Magdalene.

BACK COVER—Stone placque left in the cave by a pilgrim— *"MERCI STE MADELEINE POUR TOUS"*

Artwork depicting *Mary Magdalene Carried by Angels*

Page 23—CLOCKWISE FROM TOP LEFT—*Saint Mary Magdalene Borne by Angels* by Giulio Romano and Gianfrancesco Penni (c. 1520), Mary Magdalene clothed only in her hair, being carried to heaven by angels—one of the four lunette frescoes of the life of Mary Magdalene from the Massimi chapel of Santissima Trinità al Monte Pinco (Church of the Holy Trinity), Rome, Italy

Mary Magdalene Carried by Angels by Simon Vouet (c. 1630), Museum of Fine Arts and Archeology, Besançon, France. Musée des Beaux-Arts et d'Archéologie is the oldest public museum in France. It was set up in 1694, nearly a century before the Louvre became a public museum.

Mary Magdalene Speaking to Angels by Giotto di Bondone (c. 1320) Fresco, Magdalene Chapel, Lower Church, Basilica of Saint Francis, Assisi, Italy

Statue of Saint Mary Magdalene Carried by Angels (end of 14th century), Cathedral Basilica of St. John the Baptist and St. John the Evangelist, Toruń, Poland